# FACING YOUR FEAR OF STORMS

BY HEATHER E. SCHWARTZ

Consultant:
Tawnya M. Ward, PsyD, LP
Clinical Psychologist
Shakopee, Minnesota

**PEBBLE**
a capstone imprint

Published by Pebble, an imprint of Capstone.
1710 Roe Crest Drive, North Mankato, Minnesota 56003
capstonepub.com

Copyright © 2023 by Capstone. All rights reserved. No part of this publication may be reproduced in whole or in part, or stored in a retrieval system, or transmitted in any form or by any means, electronic, mechanical, photocopying, recording, or otherwise, without written permission of the publisher.

Library of Congress Cataloging-in-Publication Data is available on the Library of Congress website.
ISBN: 9781666355536 (hardcover)
ISBN: 9781666355598 (paperback)
ISBN: 9781666355659 (ebook PDF)

Summary: Explores the reasons why many people are afraid of storms and provides simple tips for facing this fear safely.

Editorial Credits
Editor: Christopher Harbo; Designers: Sarah Bennett and Jenny Bergstrom; Media Researcher: Svetlana Zhurkin; Production Specialist: Katy LaVigne

Image Credits
Getty Images: PeopleImages, 11; Shutterstock: all_about_people, 14, Anna Kraynova, 5, Dennis van de Water, cover, Domira (background), cover and throughout, Frame Stock Footage, 13, Good_mechanic, 17, Kapitosh (cloud), cover and throughout, kzww, 20 (middle), LightField Studios, 15, Marish (brave girl), cover and throughout, narikin, 19, Obeezyjay, 8, Pixel-Shot, 16, 20 (bottom), Rebell, 7, Serhii Hrebeniuk, 18, TY Lim, 12; Svetlana Zhurkin, 21

All internet sites appearing in back matter were available and accurate when this book was sent to press.

Printed in the United States 5236

# TABLE OF CONTENTS

A Storm Starts ................................................. 4

Crash, Crackle, Boom! ................................. 6

Storm Safety ................................................. 10

Weather the Storm ...................................... 14

Blue Skies Return ......................................... 18

    Homemade Thunder ..................... 20

    Glossary ............................................. 22

    Read More ........................................ 23

    Internet Sites ................................... 23

    Index ................................................... 24

    About the Author ........................... 24

Words in **bold** are in the glossary.

# A STORM STARTS

Dark clouds gather in the sky. Trees sway in the wind. The air smells sweet. Thunder rumbles overhead. It looks and sounds like a storm is coming.

Storms might make you feel nervous and afraid. You may feel excited too. All of those feelings are normal. But there are simple things you can do to ease your fears.

# CRASH, CRACKLE, BOOM!

Thunder and lightning are early warning signs of a storm. But why do they happen? Understanding some of the science behind storms can help keep you calm.

Lightning starts when water droplets and wind create **static electricity** in rain clouds. The static **charge** builds. Then it creates a flash of lightning.

When lightning strikes, it heats the air around it. The air **expands**, or gets larger, and makes a loud cracking sound.

The heated air starts to cool off. It **contracts**, or gets smaller, and makes a rumbling sound. That's the noise you know as thunder.

# STORM SAFETY

The best place to be during a storm is indoors. If you see lightning in the sky, move quickly. Get indoors and stay there. Do the same if you hear thunder.

If you're stuck outside, you can still stay safe. Try to find **shelter** from the rain. Keep away from metal and tall trees. They can **attract** lightning.

Planning ahead can make it easier to be sure you'll be indoors during a storm. Watch weather reports so you'll know when a storm is coming.

Stay safe from lightning while indoors too. Don't sit too close to windows. Avoid using **electronics** that are plugged in. Don't take a shower or bath until after a storm passes.

# WEATHER THE STORM

Staying busy during a storm can help pass the time. Listen to music to tune out thunder. Read a book or play a board game to keep your eyes off the skies.

A pet might like your attention too. Many animals get scared during storms. You can help by sitting with your pet and talking calmly.

If a storm has you worried, try this trick. Count the seconds between flashes of lightning and rumbles of thunder. Write down the number you reach. Every five seconds equals 1 mile (1.6 kilometers).

This trick might take time. But you will start to notice something. The number you can count to will get higher as time passes. That means the storm is moving away.

## BLUE SKIES RETURN

Storms are good for the earth. Rain waters the grass, the trees, and the fruits and vegetables we like to eat.

After a storm, all is quiet. The air might feel cool, and you may feel more relaxed. And now that you understand storms better, you will be ready for the next one.

# HOMEMADE THUNDER

Rain or shine, you can make your own thunder whenever you want. All you need are a few simple craft supplies.

## What You Need

- paper lunch bag
- crayons
- colored pencils
- markers

## What You Do

1. Think about what storms look like. Draw pictures of clouds, raindrops, and lightning on the paper lunch bag. Your storm is ready!

2. Blow into the bag to fill it with air.

3. Twist the top of the bag closed to trap the air inside.

4. Hold the bag with one hand. Now smash it into your other hand to make your own homemade thunder!

# GLOSSARY

**attention** (uh-TEN-shuhn)—playing, talking, and being with someone or something

**attract** (uh-TRAKT)—to pull something toward something else

**charge** (CHAHRJ)—an amount of electricity running through something

**contract** (kuhn-TRAKT)—to become smaller

**electronics** (i-lek-TRAH-niks)—products that run on small amounts of electricity; electronics include computers, TVs, and radios

**expand** (ik-SPAND)—to become bigger

**shelter** (SHEL-tur)—a safe, covered place

**static electricity** (STAH-tik i-lek-TRISS-uh-tee)—the buildup of an electrical charge on the surface of an object

## READ MORE

Bergin, Raymond. *Terrible Storms*. Minneapolis: Bearport Publishing, 2022.

Conrad-Stoller, Jessica. *Weather Experiments Book for Kids*. New York: Rockridge Press, 2021.

Harajli, Huda. *All About Weather*. New York: Rockridge Press, 2020.

## INTERNET SITES

*National Weather Service: Just for Kids*
weather.gov/cae/justforkids.html

*NOAA SciJinks: What Causes a Thunderstorm?*
scijinks.gov/thunderstorms-video

*The Old Farmer's Almanac for Kids*
almanac.com/kids#weather

# INDEX

feelings, 4, 16, 18

finding shelter, 10

lightning, 6, 9, 10, 13, 16

pets, 14

rain, 6, 10, 18

staying busy, 14, 16–17

staying safe, 10, 12–13

thunder, 4, 6, 9, 10, 14, 16

weather reports, 12

wind, 4, 6

# ABOUT THE AUTHOR

photo by Dan Doyle

Heather E. Schwartz has written hundreds of children's books. She enjoys watching thunderstorms while safe and dry at home. She lives in upstate New York with her husband, two kids, and two cats named Stampy and Squid.